Game On!

Relentlessly

Pursue

Your Dreams

*An Inspirational
Note-Taking Journal*

By

Nicole R. Smith

Copyright © 2020 Nicole R. Smith
All rights reserved.

Printed in the United States of America

All rights reserved. No part of this publication may be reproduced, stored in a retrieval system, or transmitted in any form or by any means—for example, electronic, photocopy, recording—without the prior written permission in writing of the author and publisher. The only exception is brief quotations in printed reviews.

The internet addresses, email addresses, and phone numbers in this book are accurate at the time of publication. They are provided as a resource. Neither Nicole R. Smith nor the publisher endorse them or vouch for their content or permanence.

Dedication Page

To dream chasers everywhere. Pursuing a goal can be exciting, exhilarating, frustrating, confusing, draining, eye-opening and liberating. Keep your head up. Take a break if you have to, but whatever you do, don't give up. A dream fulfilled is sweet to the soul. You deserve to know what that feels like. When life gets difficult, raise your head high, look the obstacle in the eye, stare it down and simply answer the challenge with a stern and determined: Game. On.

For Cyrani: To my smart, determined, resourceful, courageous beautiful college graduate. Keep pushing until you see your goal come to pass. I am here to support you along the way. Game On.

For Tony: Thank you for believing in me and being my coach along this journey.

For Mahendra: Thank you for undying, unwavering support…and not being afraid to tell me what I didn't want to hear so that the end result of this project would be amazing. Oh yeah, and thank you for reminding me to eat too.

Game On!
Relentlessly Pursue Your Dreams

This is meant to be an inspirational note-taking journal for anyone pursuing their dreams. Dream chasing is not for the faint-hearted so I commend you. This journal will encourage you to keep going, especially on the days you want to quit. Don't quit. You got this. Game On!

Committed to uplifting and encouraging dream chasers everywhere

www.nicolersmith.net/game-on
www.amazon.com/author/nicolersmith

IT ALL STARTS WITH A LEAP OF FAITH

GAME ON!

EACH DAY ADVANCES YOU ONE STEP CLOSER TO YOUR DREAMS

d

DOING EVEN ONE THING TODAY WILL BRING YOU CLOSER TO YOUR GOAL

DON'T GIVE UP

IT WON'T BE EASY, BUT IT WILL BE WORTH IT

HANG IN THERE

SUCCESS IS AROUND THE CORNER

INACTION IS THE ENEMY OF DREAMS FULFILLED

REJECTION MAKES YOU STRONGER

THERE IS NO FAILURE, JUST LESSONS LEARNED

IF IT WERE EASY, EVERYONE WOULD BE DOING IT

DO NOT UNDERESTIMATE YOUR CAPABILITIES

NO EXCUSES

IF AT FIRST YOU DON'T SUCCEED...

TRY...

TRY...

TRY...

TRY AGAIN

YOU WEAR MULTIPLE HATS WELL

WRITE THE GOAL DOWN

ASSESS WHERE YOU ARE IN THE PROCESS

SET SMALLER ATTAINABLE GOALS

MAKE A PLAN AND STICK TO IT

A GOOD ACCOUNTABILITY PARTNER GOES A LONG WAY

ALL THE GREATS HAD A COACH, YOU SHOULD HAVE ONE TOO

YOU ARE NOT IN THIS ALONE

YOU GOT THIS

COUNT THE SMALL WINS

YOU ARE ONE STEP CLOSER TO THE GOAL, KEEP GOING

CONFIDENCE LOOKS GOOD ON YOU

YOUR BEST *IS* GOOD ENOUGH

NEVER GIVE UP

CREATE A VISION BOARD

_____
_____
_____
_____
_____
_____
_____
_____
_____
_____
_____
_____
_____
_____
_____
_____
_____
_____
_____
_____
_____
_____
_____
_____

LIFE ISN'T FAIR. KEEP PUSHING ANYWAY

DO WHAT YOU CAN WITH WHAT YOU HAVE BEEN GIVEN

DON'T' GIVE UP

YOU ARE ONE STEP CLOSER TO YOUR GOAL

IT'S OK TO ASK FOR HELP

HELP SOMEONE ELSE ACCOMPLISH THEIR GOALS TOO

YOU GOT THIS

YOU CAN DO THIS

IT'S OK TO TAKE A BREAK

TRACK YOUR PROGRESS

KEEP YOUR PROMISES TO YOURSELF

YOU ARE WORTH SEEING YOUR GOAL COME TO PASS

YOU DESERVE IT

KEEP TRYING

GET UP AND TRY IT AGAIN

IT'S OK, YOU CAN'T PLEASE EVERYONE ALL THE TIME

EARLY BIRD GETS THE WORM

YOUR EARLY MORNINGS WILL PAY OFF

YOUR LATE NIGHTS WILL PAY OFF

MAKE SURE TO EAT AND SLEEP

NO SERIOUSLY, MAKE SURE YOU EAT AND SLEEP

SETBACKS PROPEL YOU FORWARD

THE RACE TO SUCCESS IS A MARATHON NOT A SPRINT

HA HA HA HA HA! LAUGH TO KEEP FROM CRYING

NEVER LET THEM SEE YOU SWEAT; MISTING, HOWEVER, IS ENCOURAGED

THEY CAN SMELL FEAR SO SPRAY ON SOME COURAGE (OR AT LEAST YOUR FAVORITE BODY SPRAY)

YOU ARE ONE STEP CLOSER THAN YOU WERE A FEW PAGES AGO

SOMETIMES YOU JUST HAVE TO START OVER

WRITE THE GOAL DOWN

ASSESS WHERE YOU ARE

ASK FOR HELP

FIND A COACH

ENVISION THE GOAL COME TO PASS

**YOU ARE WHAT YOU THINK
SO SEE YOUR GOAL ACHIEVED**

SOMETIMES YOU HAVE TO START OVER

START OVER EVEN IF IT'S THE 7TH TIME

IF AT FIRST YOU DON'T SUCCEED...

TRY AND TRY AGAIN

STAND STRONG

YOU ARE RESILIENT

SERIOUSLY, TRY AGAIN

VERY FEW PEOPLE CAN DO WHAT YOU DO SO WELL

OVERCOME SELF DOUBT

YOU ARE STEADFAST

NAVIGATE THE ROADBLOCKS AND KEEP MOVING FORWARD

WHATEVER YOU DO, DON'T GIVE UP

"NO" COULD JUST MEAN "NOT NOW"

YOU ARE DURABLE

YOU ARE TENACIOUS

YOU ARE AMAZING

YOU RISE TO THE OCCASSION

YOU ARE SMART

YOU EAT GOALS FOR BREAKFAST

FIND THE POSITIVE IN A NEGATIVE SITUATION

ADJUST THE PLAN AND KEEP MOVING FORWARD

BEWARE: EXCUSES ARE OFTEN DISGUISED AS "VALID REASONS"

PERSEVERE UNTIL THE END

YOU ARE NOT FORGOTTEN

YOU ARE PRICELESS

ARE YOU TIRED YET? TAKE A BREATH AND KEEP GOING

EVEN SETBACKS CAN OPEN DOORS

STAY THE COURSE

DON'T STOP... YOU ARE CLOSER THAN YOU THINK

NOPE, YOU ARE NOT NUTS

ENJOY AND APPRECIATE THE JOURNEY

HILLS AND VALLEYS ARE PART OF THE JOURNEY

WHO IS IN YOUR CORNER? DON'T DO THIS ALONE

ROUTE 13:19
A DREAM REALIZED IS SWEET TO THE SOUL

@nicoleRsmithnet

Nicole is a Panamanian-American, single mother, workforce development specialist, published author of Game On! Relentlessly Pursue Your Dreams, dancer, and motivational speaker. She attended Oral Roberts University on a Division I full-ride track scholarship. After graduating, she founded Step It Up! Inc., a non-profit dance organization. Her experience in sports and entertainment, radio, TV and the performing arts has spanned nearly 20 years covering the Chicago, Houston and Miami markets. She has danced and cheered for four Professional and Semi-Professional sports teams, has prepared more than 500 interns to enter the workforce and has inspired crowds upwards of 2000. In 2019, She joined the Board of the Arts and Business Council of Miami, was listed as one of WLRN's "Local Women Who Inspire You" and was selected as one of *Legacy Miami's Most Prominent and Influential Black Women In Business and Industry* and has recently becoming a contributing writer for The Life of a Single Mom.

nicoleRsmith

To order this note-taking journal and others like it:
www.amazon.com/author/nicolersmith

Made in the USA
Columbia, SC
29 October 2024